# Baby animal names

## Bobbie Kalman

🌱 Crabtree Publishing Company
www.crabtreebooks.com

# Created by Bobbie Kalman

**Author and Editor-in-Chief**
Bobbie Kalman

**Educational consultants**
Reagan Miller
Elaine Hurst
Joan King

**Editors**
Joan King
Reagan Miller
Kathy Middleton

**Proofreader**
Crystal Sikkens

**Design**
Bobbie Kalman
Katherine Berti

**Photo research**
Bobbie Kalman

**Production coordinator**
Katherine Berti

**Prepress technician**
Katherine Berti

**Photographs**
BigStockPhoto: p. 10
Other photographs by Shutterstock

**Library and Archives Canada Cataloguing in Publication**

Kalman, Bobbie, 1947-
    Baby animal names / Bobbie Kalman.

(My world)
ISBN 978-0-7787-9421-9 (bound).--ISBN 978-0-7787-9465-3 (pbk.)

    1. Animals--Infancy--Juvenile literature.
I. Title. II. Series: My world (St. Catharines, Ont.).

QL763.K34 2010          j591.3'9          C2009-906056-6

**Library of Congress Cataloging-in-Publication Data**

Kalman, Bobbie.
    Baby animal names / Bobbie Kalman.
        p. cm. -- (My world)
    ISBN 978-0-7787-9465-3 (pbk. : alk. paper) -- ISBN 978-0-7787-9421-9
(reinforced library binding : alk. paper)
    1. Animals--Infancy--Juvenile literature. I. Title. II. Series.

QL763.K355 2010
591.3'9--dc22

                                                    2009040958

## Crabtree Publishing Company

Printed in China/122009/CT20091009

www.crabtreebooks.com          1-800-387-7650

**Published in Canada**
**Crabtree Publishing**
616 Welland Ave.
St. Catharines, Ontario
L2M 5V6

**Published in the United States**
**Crabtree Publishing**
PMB 59051
350 Fifth Avenue, 59th Floor
New York, New York 10118

**Published in the United Kingdom**
**Crabtree Publishing**
Maritime House
Basin Road North, Hove
BN41 1WR

**Published in Australia**
**Crabtree Publishing**
386 Mt. Alexander Rd.
Ascot Vale (Melbourne)
VIC 3032

# Words to know

pouch

bear    fox kit    goat    kangaroo
cub    or pup    kid    joey

koala    raccoon    wolf
joey    kittens    cub

# Children are called **kids**.

# Baby **goats** are called kids, too.

Baby **cats** are called **kittens**.

Did you know that baby **raccoons** are called kittens, too?

# A baby **dog** is called a **puppy**.

Did you know that a baby **fox** is called a **pup** or a **kit**?

Did you know that a baby **wolf** is called a pup or a **cub**?

Did you know that a baby **bear** is also called a cub?

A baby **kangaroo** is called a **joey**.
The joey lives in its mother's **pouch**.

pouch

Did you know that a baby **koala**
is called a joey, too?
The baby koala also lives
in its mother's pouch.

## Activity

How many baby animal names do you know?

A baby horse is called a **foal**.

A baby rabbit is called a **bunny**.

A baby sheep
is called a **lamb**.

A baby deer
is called a **fawn**.

A baby giraffe
is called a **calf**.

# Notes for adults

## What's in a name?
*Baby animal names* helps children learn the names of animals and what they are called as babies. Ask the children if they think baby goats are like children and if raccoons are like cats, since they share the same baby names. Make a list of all the nicknames the children were called when they were babies.

## Animal match-ups
Create an animal match-up game to help reinforce new animal vocabulary and place memory. Create a set of cards with pictures showing the baby animals in the book. On a separate set of cards, write the name of the baby animal (kit, joey, cub, foal, calf). Lay out the cards face down on the floor. Ask the students to take turns turning over two cards to make as many matches as they can.

*It's Fun to Learn about Baby Animals Series contains wonderful books about baby animals that introduce children to animal families, species, life cycles, and many more concepts.*
***Guided Reading: J***

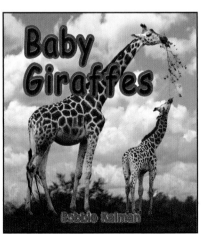

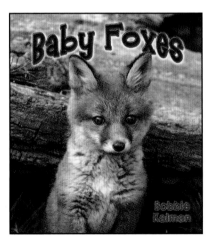